Why don't those damned oil companies fly their own flags on their personal property—maybe a flag with a gas pump on it.

—Brigadier General Smedley D. Butler,
1937

ISBN: 0-922915-86-5
ISBN-13: 978-0-922915-86-6

Feral House
1240 W. Sims Way Suite 124
Port Townsend, WA 98368

www.FeralHouse.com
info@feralhouse.com

The publisher wishes to thank Molly Swanton and the Butler family for their understanding and assistance, Jeff Roth for long-lost wire photos, Bill Nelson for tracking down excellent material, Hedi and Michael for their assistance, and Dr. James J. Martin for his telephone lessons on American anti-interventionist publishing.

Brigadier General Smedley Darlington Butler
and Three Foot Soldiers.

This photograph hangs on the Butler family's wall today.
(Photo courtesy Molly Swanton)

WAR IS A RACKET

by Smedley D. Butler

The antiwar classic by America's most decorated general,
two other anti-interventionist tracts,
and photographs from *The Horror of It: Camera Records of War's Gruesome Glories*

Introductions by
Adam Parfrey

fh

TABLE OF CONTENTS

Smedley Butler addresses Bonus Marchers in Washington, D.C., urging them to remain in camp until they receive their "adjusted compensation certificates."

AP photo wire, July 24, 1932.
(Courtesy of Jeff Roth)

INTRODUCTION

HOW A MILITARY HERO BLEW THE WHISTLE ON CORPORATE MALFEASANCE

BY ADAM PARFREY

In early to mid-20th century Latin America, the citizens of country after country heard the rhetoric of [President Woodrow] Wilson but came up hard against the practices of American mining, agriculture and construction giants; and children though they may have been in the eyes of both the paternalistic Wilson and the far more sinister corporate magnates, those people understood the game that was being played out within their borders.

—Caleb Carr, *The New York Observer*, in an (4/14/03) article spanking the interventionism of President Bush's neo-Conservative cabinet.

The U.S. government thanked the efforts of World War I soldiers with a "war bonus" of approximately $1,000 to be paid late as 1945. But as Great Depression and the Dust Bowl misery touched the continental states, unemployed veterans desired to have their bonus paid sooner. In May 1932 out-of-work vets arrived in Washington D.C. to impress their bonus pleas to Congress. A pro-bonus bill sponsored by Wright Patman was threatened veto by President Hoover and overturned House passage by a Republican Senate. As tens of thousands of Hooverville-occupying vets demonstrated their discontent in a "death march," Generals George Patton and Douglas MacArthur moved in on the veterans with a fresher contingent of the U.S. Army. Two died, including an infant, and hundreds of veterans were injured, in MacArthur's successful attempt to "gain control" of D.C.

The Bonus Marchers' primary upper-ranked supporter? Smedley D. Butler, the Brigadier General who was twice awarded the Medal of Honor and once the so-called "Brevet medal," when the Medal of Honor was not given officers. Known for his fair play to soldiers regardless of rank, Butler's support of the "Bonus Marchers" helped boost the desperate foot-soldiers' movement. The Brigadier General's disparaging of the mass media and "big business" was particularly popular in the Depression. But those same big business interests, buoyed by the ability of Italian Fascist "Corporatism" to turn back labor demands in the restructuring of its economy, took special note of Butler's support from a half-million veterans, which would have made an intimidating force against FDR and his hated New Deal, and his elimination of the gold standard. But as far as Smedley Butler was concerned, "I believe in making Wall Street pay for it [the bonuses]—taking Wall Street by the throat and shaking it up."

As a Marine officer, Butler oversaw American forays into China, Nicaragua, Cuba and Haiti, and this is where he picked up his frequently expressed opinion that he was no more than a bully boy for American corporations. Butler's skepticism about the U.S. government may have been partly the result of his Quaker background. During the Prohibition, Butler was made Police Chief of the mob-plagued city of Philadelphia in 1924 and 1925 where in a non-war interlude he effectively moved against open saloons, bars and speakeasies. Mass magazines, like the early diet and fitness periodical *Strength* (March 1924 issue), featured Butler's military-type run against the Philly "gangsters."

GENERAL BUTLER'S IRON GRIP

Courage is Strength, Ditto Unswerving Purpose—That is Why Philadelphia's Crooks and Bootleggers Flee From the Mailed Fist of "Old Hell's Devil Butler." You've read much, perhaps, of the great heroes of fiction. Perhaps they were not all great heroes. Some of them may have been just ordinary leading characters, knights errant, adventurers, soldiers of fortune. Probably you've

> admired them, thrilled to their deeds, longed to emulate them, and possibly got just a wee bit tired of them all with their calm, piercing and various other kinds of eyes, their tremendous energy and all that sort of thing.
>
> How would you like to meet one of them? A lot of Philadelphians have just had that opportunity, and a great many of them didn't care for it one bit. Of course, you know we are referring to Brigadier General Smedley D. Butler of the United States Marine Corps, who has just recently been appointed Director of the Department of Public Safety in the Quaker City.
>
> —T. Von Ziekursch, *Strength* magazine, March 1924

In a 1931 speech, Butler recounted a story about Italian Prime Minister Benito Mussolini, how he had run over a child with his car, and said, as he moved on, "It was only one life. What is one life in the affairs of the State." This remark caused a great commotion among U.S. authorities after Mussolini strongly denied the episode, and Butler was quickly placed under arrest and ordered court-martialed by President Hoover. Pre-World War II worship of Italian Fascism in America can be seen in the July 1934 issue of *Fortune* magazine, which celebrated the Italian corporatist state. Due to hostile public reaction, the court-martial against Butler was dropped entirely. The Brigadier General soon after announced his retirement in the *Liberty* magazine article "To Hell with the Admirals! Why I Retired at Fifty."

When he no longer wished to be known as a "racketeer for capitalism," Butler became a widely-quoted spokesman for constitutional American principles over imperialist American practice. Lowell Thomas, the famous journalist widely known for making a British Liaison to the Arab revolt of World War I "Lawrence of Arabia," took on "The Adventures of Smedley D. Butler" in the 1933 book, *Old Gimlet Eye*, complete with endpaper illustrations of Smedley putting down revolting, barefoot sword-wielding Haitians with pistol and rifle.

The subtitle of this edition is not entirely accurate, as Smedley Butler was not an "antiwar" activist so much as an isolationist. And he died on June 21, 1940, months prior to the attack on Pearl Harbor. Within the pages of *War Is a Racket*, Butler said that the U.S. "should build an ironclad defense a rat couldn't crawl through."

On the other hand, Butler also invoked against capitalist greed: "I helped make Mexico, especially Tampico, safe for American oil interests in 1914. I helped make Haiti and Cuba a decent place for the National City Bank boys to collect revenues in. I helped in the raping of half a dozen Central American republics for the benefits of Wall Street. The record of racketeering is long. I helped purify Nicaragua for the international banking house of Brown Brothers in 1909–1912. I brought light to the Dominican Republic for American sugar interests in 1916. In China I helped to see to it that Standard Oil went its way unmolested." Strangely enough, *Reader's Digest* saw fit to condense *War Is A Racket* as a book supplement.

Lowell Thomas says in his introduction to the *Reader's Digest* version of *War Is A Racket*:

> Even his opponents concede that in his stand on public questions, General Butler has been motivated by the same fiery integrity and loyal patriotism which has distinguished his service in countless Marine campaigns.

But the view that opponents forever saw integrity in Butler's "public questions" overlooked the *New York Times* and *Time* Magazine's public lancing when Butler revealed a "Wall Street Plot to Seize the Government"—investigated, confirmed (and partially suppressed) by the McCormack-Dickstein Congressional Committee—that American Legion leaders and well-known men of Wall Street, one a major attorney for J.P. Morgan & Co., had planned the first American fascist dictatorship.

Time Magazine (at the time controlled by J.P. Morgan & Co.), said, under a first-page headline on December 3, 1934, "PLOT WITHOUT PLOTTERS":

> Such as the nightmarish page of future United States history pictured last week in Manhattan by General Butler himself to the special House Committee investigating Un-American Activities. No military officer of the United States since the late tempestuous George Custer has succeeded in publicly floundering in so much hot water as Smedley Darlington Butler...
>
> General Butler's sensational tongue had not been

> heard in the nation's press for more than a week when he cornered a reporter for the *Philadelphia Record* and the *New York Post,* poured into his ears the lurid tale that he had been offered leadership of a Fascist Putsch scheduled for next year...
>
> Thanking their stars for having such sure-fire publicity dropped in their laps, Representatives McCormack and Dickstein began calling witnesses to expose the "plot." But there did not seem to be any plotters...
>
> Mr. Morgan, just off a boat from Europe, had nothing to say but partner Lamont did: "Perfect moonshine! Too utterably ridiculous to comment upon!!..."

As George Seldes put it in his 1947 book *1000 Americans,* "Any reader comparing the testimony and the Committee report on this event ... must conclude that the *Time* report consists of distortion and propaganda."

In his long out-of-print 1973 tome, *The Plot to Seize the White House,* Jules Archer shows how the *New York Times* denigrated Butler's whistle-blowing and vastly underplayed the reality of the Congressional inquiry. Its November 21, 1934 headline said, hostile quote marks retained:

GEN. BUTLER BARES 'FASCIST PLOT'
TO SEIZE GOVERNMENT BY FORCE

> *Says Bond Salesman, as Representative of Wall St. Group, Asked Him to Lead Army of 500,000 in March on Capital—Those Named Make Angry Denials—Dickstein Gets Charge*

The complex saga behind the coup attempt, and the devious manner in which Butler was solicited to join the attempt to intimidate President Roosevelt into functional inactivity, was strikingly described by Archer in *The Plot to Seize the White House* (Hawthorn Books, 1973) and a bit less provocatively by a History Channel documentary titled *The Plot to Overthrow FDR* (available on videotape from International Historic Films, www.ihffilm.com/ihf/r547.html).

The most revealing details of the McCormack/Dickstein Committee report were suppressed in its original release. Though the report confirmed Smedley Butler's revelation of outrageous corporate plots, it failed to detail the names of prominent corporate entities, whose mention would have embarrassed the politicians they supported and the "patriotic" groups they helped form. Only after George Seldes released his obscure book, *1000 Americans*, did their suppressed names come to light in two revealing appendices, reproduced below.

From *1000 Americans*, © 1947 by George Seldes. Appendix 20:

THE FIRST FASCIST PLOT TO SEIZE THE U.S. GOVERNMENT

> *[Seldes' Editorial Note: General Smedley Butler testified before a Congressional Committee that several Wall Street bankers, one of them connected with J.P. Morgan and Co., several founders of the American Liberty League, and several heads of the American Legion plotted to seize the government of the United States shortly after President Roosevelt established the New Deal. The press, with a few exceptions, suppressed the news. Worse yet, the McCormack-Dickstein Committee suppressed the facts involving the big business interests, although it confirmed the plot which newspapers and magazines had either refused to mention or had tried to kill by ridicule. In the following quotations the suppressed parts are in italics.]*

General Butler's Testimony regarding his interview with Gerald G. MacGuire, of the brokerage firm of Grayson M.P. Murphy:

> Then MacGuire said that he was the chairman of the distinguished-guest committee of the American Legion, on Louis Johnson's staff; that Louis Johnson had, at MacGuire's suggestion, put my name down to be incited as a distinguished guest of the Chicago convention; that Johnson had then taken this list, presented by MacGuire

of distinguished guests, to the White House for approval; that Louis Howe, one of the secretaries to the President, had crossed my name off and said that I was not to be invited—that the President would not have it.

I thought I smelled a rat, right away—that they were trying to get me mad—to get my goat. I said nothing.

"He (Murphy) is on our side, though. He wants to see the soldiers cared for.

"Is he responsible, too, for making the Legion a strikebreaking outfit?"

"No, no. He does not control anything in the Legion now."

I said: "You know very well that it is nothing but a strikebreaking outfit used by capital for that purpose and that is the reason we have all those big clubhouses and that is the reason I pulled out from it. They have been using these dumb soldiers to break strikes."

He said: "Murphy hasn't anything to do with that. He is a very fine fellow."

I said, "I do not doubt that, but there is some reason for his putting $125,000 into this."

Well, that was the end of that conversation.

I said, "Is there anything stirring about it yet?"

"Yes," he says: "you watch; in two or three weeks you will see it come out in the papers. There will be big fellows in it"... and in about two weeks the American Liberty League appeared, which just about what he described it to be. We might have an assistant President, somebody to take the blame; and if things do not work out, he can drop him.

He said, "That is what he was building up Hugh Johnson for. Hugh Johnson talked too damn much and got him into a hole, and he is going to fire him in the next three or four weeks."

I said, "How do you know all this?"

"Oh," he said, "we are in with him all the time. We know what is going to happen."

General Butler's testimony of his interview with Robert Sterling Clark:

He (Clark) laughed and said, "That speech cost a lot of money." Clark told me that it had cost him a lot of money. Now either from what he said then or from what MacGuire had said, I got the impression that the speech had been written by John W. Davis—one or the other of them told me that—but he thought it was a big joke that these fellows were claiming the authority of that speech...

He said, "When I was in Paris, my headquarters were Morgan & Hodges (Harjes). We had a meeting over there. I might as well tell you that our group is for you, for the head of this organization. Morgan & Hodges (Harjes) are against you. The Morgan interests say that you cannot be trusted, that you are too radical, you cannot be trusted. They are for Douglas MacArthur as the head of it. Douglas MacArthur's term expires in November, and if he is not reappointed it is to be presumed that he will be disappointed and sore and they are for getting him to head it."

I said, "I do not think that you will get the soldiers to follow him, Jerry... He is in bad odor, because he put on a uniform with medals to march down the street in Washington, I know the soldiers."

"Well, then, we will get Hanford MacNider. They want either MacArthur or MacNider... They do not want you. But our group tell us you are the only fellow in America who can get the soldiers together. They say, 'Yes, but he will get them together and go the wrong way.' That is what they say if you take charge of them."

I said, "MacNider won't do either. He will not get the soldiers to follow him, because he has been opposed to the bonus."

"Yes, but we will have him change."

And it is interesting to note that three weeks later after this conversation MacNider changed and turned around for the bonus. It is interesting to note that.

He said, "There is going to be a big quarrel over the reappointment of MacArthur" and he said, "You watch the President reappoint him. He is going to go right and if he does not reappoint him, he is going to go left."

> I have been watching with a great deal of interest this quarrel over his reappointment to see how it comes out. He said, "You know as well as I do that MacArthur is Stotesbury's son-in-law in Philadelphia—Morgan's representative in Philadelphia. You just see how it goes and if I am not telling you the truth."
>
> I noticed that MacNider turned around for the bonus, and that there is a row over the reappointment of MacArthur. So he left me saying, "I am going down to Miami..."

Testimony of Paul Comly French of *Philadelphia Record,* in the Smedley Butler-Legion hearing:

> At first he (MacGuire) suggested that the General (Butler) organize this outfit himself and ask a dollar a year dues from everybody. We discussed that, and then he came around to the point of getting outside financial funds, and he said it would not be any trouble to raise a million dollars. He said he could go to John W. Davis (attorney for J.P. Morgan and Co.) or Perkins of the National City Bank, and any number of persons to get it.
>
> Of course, that may or may not mean anything. That is, his reference to John W. Davis and Perkins of the National City Bank. During my conversation with him I did not of course commit to the General to anything. I was just feeling him along. Later, we discussed the question of arms and equipment, and he suggested that they could be obtained from the Remington Arms Co., on credit through the DuPonts.
>
> I do not think at that time he mentioned the connection of DuPonts with the American Liberty League, but he skirted all around it. That is, I do not think he mentioned the Liberty League, but he skirted all around the idea that that was the back door; one of the DuPonts is on the board of directors of the American Liberty League and they own a controlling interest in the Remington Arms Co... He said the General would not have any trouble enlisting 500,000 men.

From *1000 Americans*, © 1947 by George Seldes. Appendix 21:

THE FASCIST PLOT OFFICIALLY CONFIRMED

74th Congress, 1st Session House of Representatives Report No. 153 Investigation of Nazi and Other Propaganda February 15, 1935–Committed to the Committee of the Whole House on the state of the Union and ordered to be printed

Mr. McCormack, from the committee appointed to investigate Nazi and other propaganda, submitted the following REPORT (Pursuant to House Resolution No. 198, 73rd Congress) Fascism

There have been isolated cases of activity by organizations which seemed to be guided by fascist principle, which the committee investigated and found that they had made no progress...

In the last few weeks of the committee's official life it received evidence showing that certain persons had made an attempt to establish a fascist organization in this country. No evidence was presented and this committee had none to show a connection between this effort and any fascist activity of any European country.

There is no question that these attempts were discussed, were planned, and might have been placed in execution when and if the financial backers deemed it expedient.

This committee received evidence from Maj. Gen. Smedley D. Butler (retired), twice decorated by the Congress of the United States. He testified before the committee as to conversations with one Gerald C. MacGuire in which the latter is alleged to have suggested the formation of a fascist army under the leadership of General Butler (p. 8-114 D.C. 6 II).

MacGuire denied these allegations under oath, but your committee was able to verify all the pertinent

> statements made by General Butler, with the exception of the direct statement suggesting the creation of the organization. This, however, was corroborated in the correspondence of MacGuire with his principal, Robert Sterling Clark, of New York City, while MacGuire was abroad studying the various forms of veterans' organizations of Fascist character (p. 111 D.C. 6 II).

The following is an excerpt from one of MacGuire's letters:

> *I had a very interesting talk last evening with a man who is quite well up on affairs here and he seems to be of the opinion that the* Croix de Feu *will be very patriotic during this crisis and will take the cuts or be the moving spirit in the veterans to accept the cuts. Therefore they will, in all probability, be in opposition to the Socialists and functionaries. The general spirit among the functionaries seems to be that the correct way to regain recovery is to spend more money and increase wages, rather than to put more people out of work and cut salaries.*
>
> *The* Croix de Feu *is getting a great number of new recruits, and I recently attended a meeting of this organization and was quite impressed with the type of men belonging. These fellows are interested only in the salvation of France, and I feel sure that the country could not be in better hands because they are not politicians, they are a cross-section of the best people of the country from all walks of life, people who gave their "all" between 1914 and 1918 that France might be saved, and I feel sure that if a crucial test ever comes to the Republic that these men will be the bulwark upon which France will be served.*
>
> *There may be more uprisings, there may be more difficulties, but as is evidenced right now when the emergency arises and part difficulties are forgotten as far as France is concerned, and all become united in the one desire and purpose to keep this country as it is, the most democratic, and the country of the greatest freedom on the European Continent (p. III D.C. 6 II).*

> *This committee asserts that any efforts based on lines as suggested in the foregoing and leading off to the extreme right, are just as bad as efforts which would lead to the extreme left.*
>
> *Armed forces for the purpose of establishing a dictatorship by means of Fascism or a dictatorship through the instrumentality of the proletariat, or a dictatorship predicated in part on racial and religious hatreds, have no place in this country.*

Smedley Butler helped destroy a corporate Fascist Putsch in the mid-1930s, but how long did that last? In the 1960s, all four primary liberal leaders were assassinated. In the mid-'90s, a so-called Democrat President turned back the Bill of Rights and Constitution with a multitude of crime bills. And in the year 2000, Jim Crow laws were revived, and a Presidential election was swayed by disallowing over 50,000 eligible African-Americans to vote in the state of Florida. Corporations will not be denied their sway and profit. Regardless of one's political affiliation, *War Is A Racket* remains an astonishing reminder that America once stood for constitutional principles and not power-enhanced greed mongering.

Burning Hooverville

A photo opportunity emphasizing Smedley Butler's desire to sweep clean dirty government stables.

From Times Wide World Archives, April 19, 1932.
(Courtesy Jeff Roth)

WAR IS A RACKET

by Smedley D. Butler
Major General,
United States Marines

(Originally published
by Round Table Press, Inc.,
New York, 1935)

CHAPTER ONE

WAR IS A RACKET

WAR is a racket. It always has been. It is possibly the oldest, easily the most profitable, surely the most vicious. It is the only one international in scope. It is the only one in which the profits are reckoned in dollars and the losses in lives.

A racket is best described, I believe, as something that is not what it seems to the majority of people. Only a small "inside" group knows what it is about. It is conducted for the benefit of the very few, at the expense of the very many. Out of war a few people make huge fortunes.

In the World War a mere handful garnered the profits of the conflict. At least 21,000 new millionaires and billionaires were made in the United States during the World War. That many admitted their huge blood gains in their income tax returns. How many other war millionaires falsified their income tax returns no one knows.

How many of these war millionaires shouldered a rifle? How many of them dug a trench? How many of them knew what it meant to go hungry in a rat-infested dugout? How many of them spent sleepless, frightened nights, ducking shells and shrapnel and machine gun bullets? How many of them parried the bayonet thrust of an enemy? How many of them were wounded or killed in battle?

Out of war nations acquire additional territory, if they are victorious. They just take it. This newly acquired territory promptly is exploited by the few—the self-same few who wrung dollars out of blood in the war. The general public shoulders the bill.

And what is this bill?

This bill renders a horrible accounting. Newly placed gravestones. Mangled bodies. Shattered minds. Broken hearts and homes. Economic instability. Depression and all its attendant miseries. Back-breaking taxation for generations and generations.

For a great many years, as a soldier, I had a suspicion that war was a racket; not until I retired to civil life did I fully realize it. Now that I see the international war clouds again gathering, as they are today, I must face it and speak out.

Again they are choosing sides. France and Russia met and agreed to stand side by side. Italy and Austria hurried to make a similar agreement. Poland and Germany cast sheep's eyes at each other, forgetting, for the nonce, their dispute over the Polish Corridor. The assassination of King Alexander of Yugoslavia complicated matters. Yugoslavia and Hungary, long bitter enemies, were almost at each other's throats. Italy was ready to jump in. But France was waiting. So was Czechoslovakia. All of them are looking ahead to war. Not the people—not those who fight and pay and die—only those who foment wars and remain safely at home to profit.

There are 40,000,000 men under arms in the world today, and our statesmen and diplomats have the temerity to say that war is not in the making.

Hell's bells! Are these 40,000,000 men being trained to be dancers?

Not in Italy, to be sure. Premier Mussolini knows what they are being trained for. He, at least, is frank enough to speak out. Only the other day, Il Duce in "International Conciliation," the publication of the Carnegie Endowment for International Peace, said:

> *And, above all, Fascism, the more it considers and observes the future and the development of humanity quite apart from political considerations of the moment, believes neither in the possibility for the utility of perpetual peace... War alone brings up to its highest tension all human energy and puts the stamp of nobility upon the peoples who have the courage to meet it.*

Undoubtedly Mussolini means exactly what he says. His well trained army, his great fleet of planes, and even his navy are ready for war—anxious for it, apparently. His recent stand at the side of Hungary in the latter's dispute with Yugoslavia showed that. And the hurried mobilization of his troops on the Austrian border after the assassination of Dollfuss showed it too. There are others in Europe too whose sabre-rattling presages war, sooner or later.

Herr Hitler, with his rearming Germany and his constant demands for more and more arms, is an equal if not a greater menace to peace. France only recently increased the term of military service for its youth from a year to eighteen months.

Yes, all over, nations are camping on their arms. The mad dogs of Europe are on the loose.

In the Orient the maneuvering is more adroit. Back in 1904, when Russian and Japan fought, we kicked out our old friends the Russians and backed Japan. Then our very generous international bankers were financing Japan. Now the trend is to poison us against the Japanese. What does the "open door" policy in China mean to us? Our trade with China is about $90,000,000 a year. Or the Philippine Islands? We have spent about $600,000,000 in the Philippines in 35 years and we (our bankers and industrialists and speculators) have private investments there of less than $200,000.

Then, to save that China trade of about $90,000,000, or to protect these private investments of less than $200,000,000 in the Philippines, we would be all stirred up to hate Japan and go to war—a war that might well cost us tens of billions of dollars, hundreds of thousands of lives of Americans, and many more hundreds of thousands of physically maimed and mentally unbalanced men.

Of course, for this loss, there would be a compensating profit—fortunes would be made. Millions and billions of dollars would be piled up. By a few. Munitions makers. Ship builders. Manufacturers. Meat packers. Speculators. They would fare well.

Yes, they are getting ready for another war. Why shouldn't they? It pays high dividends.

But what does it profit the masses?

What does it profit the men who are killed? What does it profit the men who are maimed? What does it profit their mothers and sisters, their wives and their sweethearts? What does it profit their children?

What does it profit anyone except the very few to whom war means huge profits?

Yes, and what does it profit the nation?

Take our own case. Until 1898 we didn't own a bit of territory outside the mainland of North America. At that time our national debt was a little more than $1,000,000,000. Then we became "internationally minded." We forgot, or shunted aside, the advice of the Father of our Country. We forgot Washington's warning about "entangling alliances." We went to war. We acquired outside territory. At the end of the World War period, as a direct result of our fiddling in international affairs, our national debt had jumped to over $25,000,000,000. Therefore, on a purely financial bookkeeping basis, we ran a little behind year for year, and that foreign trade might well have been ours without the wars.

It would have been far cheaper (not to say safer) for the average American who pays the bills to stay out of foreign entanglements. For a very few this racket, like bootlegging and other underworld rackets, brings fancy profits, but the cost of operations is always transferred to the people—who do not profit.

CHAPTER TWO

WHO MAKES THE PROFITS?

The World War, rather our brief participation in it, has cost the United States some $52,000,000,000. Figure it out. That means $400 to every American man, woman, and child. And we haven't paid the debt yet. We are paying it, our children will pay it, and our children's children probably still will be paying the cost of that war.

The normal profits of a business concern in the United States are six, eight, ten, and sometimes even twelve per cent. But wartime profits—ah! that is another matter—twenty, sixty, one hundred, three hundred, and even eighteen hundred per cent—the sky is the limit. All that the traffic will bear. Uncle Sam has the money. Let's get it.

Of course, it isn't put that crudely in war time. It is dressed into speeches about patriotism, love of country, and "we must all put our shoulder to the wheel," but the profits jump and leap and skyrocket—and are safely pocketed. Let's just take a few examples:

Take our friend the du Ponts, the powder people—didn't one of them testify before a Senate committee recently that their powder won the war? Or something? How did they do in the war? They were a patriotic corporation. Well, the average earnings of the du Ponts for the period 1910 to 1914 was $6,000,000 a year. It wasn't much, but the du Ponts managed to get along on it. Now let's look at their average yearly profit during the war years, 1914 to 1918. Fifty-eight million dollars a year profit, we find! Nearly ten times that of normal times, and the profits of normal times were pretty good. An increase in profits of more than 950 per cent.

Take one of our little steel companies that so patriotically shunted aside the making of rails and girders and bridges to manufacture war materials. Well, their 1910–1914 yearly earnings averaged $6,000,000. Then came the war. And, like loyal citizens, Bethlehem Steel promptly turned to munitions making. Did their profits jump—or did they let Uncle

Sam in for a bargain? Well, their 1914–1918 average was $49,000,000 a year!

Or, let's take United States Steel. The normal earnings during the five-year period prior to the war were $105,000,000 a year. Not bad. Then along came the war and up went the profits. The average yearly profit for the period 1914–1918 was $240,000,000. Not bad.

There you have some of the steel and powder earnings. Let's look at something else. A little copper, perhaps. That always does well in war times.

Anaconda, for instance. Average yearly earnings during the pre-war years 1910–1914 of $10,000,000. During the war years 1914–1918 profits leaped to $34,000,000 per year.

Or Utah Copper. Average of $5,000,000 per year during the 1910–1914 period. Jumped to average of $21,000,000 yearly profits for the war period.

Let's group these five, with three smaller companies. The total yearly average profits of the pre-war period 1910–1914 were $137,480,000. Then along came the war. The yearly average profits for this group skyrocketed to $408,300,000.

A little increase in profits of approximately 200 per cent.

Does war pay? It paid them. But they aren't the only ones. There are still others. Let's take leather.

For the three-year period before the war the total profits of Central Leather Company were $3,500,000. That was approximately $1,167,000 a year. Well, in 1916 Central Leather returned a profit of $15,500,000, a small increase of 1,100 per cent. That's all. The General Chemical Company averaged a profit for the three years before the war of a little over $800,000 a year. Then came the war, and the profits jumped to $12,000,000. A leap of 1,400 per cent.

International Nickel Company—and you can't have a war without nickel—showed an increase in profits from a mere average of $4,000,000 a year to $73,500,000 yearly. Not bad? An increase of more than 1,700 per cent.

American Sugar Refining Company averaged $200,000 a year for the three years before the war. In 1916 a profit of $6,000,000 was recorded.

Listen to Senate Document No. 259. The Sixty-Fifth Congress, reporting on corporate earnings and government revenues. Considering the profits of 122 meat packers, 153 cotton manufactures, 299 garment makers, 49 steel plants, and 340 coal producers during the war. Profits under 25 per cent were exceptional. For instance, the coal companies made between 100 per cent and 7,856 per cent on their capital stock during the war. The Chicago packers doubled and tripled their earnings.

And let us not forget the bankers who financed this great war. If anyone had the cream of the profits it was the bankers. Being partnerships rather than incorporated organization, they do not have to report to stockholders. And their profits were as secret as they were immense. How the bankers made their millions and their billions I do not know, because those little secrets never become public—even before a Senate investigatory body.

But here's how some of the other patriotic industrialists and speculators chiseled their way into war profits.

Take the shoe people. They like war. It brings business with abnormal profits. They made huge profits on sales abroad to our allies. Perhaps, like the munitions manufacturers and armament makers, they also sold to the enemy. For a dollar is a dollar whether it comes from Germany or from France. But they did well by Uncle Sam too. For instance, they sold Uncle Sam 35,000,000 pairs of hobnailed service shoes. There were 4,000,000 soldiers. Eight pairs, and more, to a soldier. My regiment during the war had only a pair to a soldier. Some of these shoes probably are still in existence. They were good shoes. But when the war was over Uncle Sam had a matter of 25,000,000 pairs left over. Bought—and paid for. Profits recorded and pocketed.

There was still lots of leather left. So the leather people sold your Uncle Sam hundreds of thousands of McClellan saddles for the cavalry. But there wasn't any American cavalry overseas! Somebody had to get rid of this leather, however. Somebody had to make a profit on it—so we had a lot of those McClellan saddles. And we probably have those yet.

Also somebody had a lot of mosquito netting. They sold your Uncle Sam 20,000,000 mosquito nets for the use of the soldiers overseas. I suppose the boys were expected to put it over them as they tried to sleep in the muddy trenches—one hand scratching cooties on their backs and the other making passes at scurrying rats. Well, not one of these mosquito nets ever got to France!

Anyhow, these thoughtful manufacturers wanted to make sure that no soldier would be without his mosquito net, so 40,000,000 additional yards of mosquito netting were sold to Uncle Sam.

There were pretty good profits in mosquito netting in war days, even if there were no mosquitoes in France.

I suppose, if the war had lasted just a little longer, the enterprising mosquito netting manufacturers would have sold your Uncle Sam a couple of consignments of mosquitoes to plant in France so that more mosquito netting would be in order.

Airplane and engine manufacturers felt they, too, should get their just profits out of this war. Why not? Everybody else was getting theirs. So $1,000,000,000—count them if you live long enough—was spent by Uncle Sam in building airplanes and airplane engines that never left the ground! Not one plane, or motor, out of the billion dollars' worth ordered, ever got into a battle in France. Just the same the manufacturers made their little profit of 30, 100 or perhaps 300 per cent.

Undershirts for soldiers cost 14 cents to make and Uncle Sam paid 30 cents to 40 cents each for them—a nice little profit for the undershirt manufacturer. And the stocking manufacturers and the uniform manufacturers and the cap manufacturers and the steel helmet manufacturers—all got theirs.

Why, when the war was over some 4,000,000 sets of equipment—knapsacks and the things that go to fill them—crammed warehouses on this side. Now they are being scrapped because the regulations have changed the contents. But the manufacturers collected their wartime profits on them—and they will do it all over again the next time.

There were lots of brilliant ideas for profit making during the war.

One very versatile patriot sold Uncle Sam twelve dozen 48-inch wrenches. Oh, they were very nice wrenches. The only trouble was that there was only one nut ever made that was large enough for these wrenches. That is the one that holds the turbines at Niagara Falls! Well, after Uncle Sam had bought them and the manufacturer had pocketed the profit, the wrenches were put on freight cars and shunted all around the United States in an effort to find a use for them. When the Armistice was signed it was indeed a sad blow to the wrench manufacturer. He was just about to make some nuts to fit the wrenches. Then he planned to sell these, too, to your Uncle Sam.

Still another had the brilliant idea that colonels shouldn't ride in automobiles, nor should they even ride horseback. One had probably seen a picture of Andy Jackson riding on a buckboard. Well, some 6,000 buckboards were sold to Uncle Sam for the use of colonels! Not one of them was used. But the buckboard manufacturer got his war profit.

The shipbuilders felt they should come in on some of it, too. They built a lot of ships that made a lot of profit. More than $3,000,000,000 worth. Some of the ships were all right. But $635,000,000 worth of them were made of wood and wouldn't float! The seams opened up—and they sank. We paid for them, though. And somebody pocketed the profits.

It has been estimated by statisticians and economists and researchers that the war cost your Uncle Sam $52,000,000,000. Of this sum, $39,000,000,000 was expended in the actual war period. This expenditure yielded $16,000,000,000 in profits. That is how the 21,000 billionaires and millionaires got that way. This $16,000,000,000 profits is not to be sneezed at. It is quite a tidy sum. And it went to a very few.

The Senate (Nye) committee probe of the munitions industry and its wartime profits, despite its sensational disclosures, hardly has scratched the surface.

Even so, it has had some effect. The State Department has been studying "for some time" methods of keeping out of war. The War Department suddenly decides it has a wonderful plan to spring. The Administration names a committee—with the War and Navy Departments ably represented under the chairmanship of a Wall Street speculator—to limit profits in war time. To what extent isn't suggested. Hmmm. Possibly the profits of 300 and 600 and 1,600 per cent of those who turned blood into gold in the World War would be limited to some smaller figure.

Apparently, however, the plan does not call for any limitation of losses—that is, the losses of those who fight the war. As far as I have been able to ascertain there is nothing in the scheme to limit a soldier to the loss of but one eye, or one arm, or to limit his wounds to one or two or three. Or to limit the loss of life.

There is nothing in this scheme, apparently, that says not more than twelve per cent of a regiment shall be wounded in battle, or that not more than seven per cent in a division should be killed.

Of course, the committee cannot be bothered with such trifling matters.

CHAPTER THREE

WHO PAYS THE BILLS?

WHO provides the profits—these nice little profits of 20, 100, 300, 1,500, and 1,800 per cent? We all pay them—in taxation. We paid the bankers their profits when we bought Liberty Bonds at $100 and sold them back at $84 or $86 to the banker. These bankers collected $100 plus. It was a simple manipulation. The bankers control the security marts. It was easy for them to depress the price of these bonds. Then all of us—the people—got frightened and sold the bonds at $84 or $86. The bankers bought them. Then these same bankers stimulated a boom and government bonds went to par—and above. Then the bankers collected their profits.

But the soldier pays the biggest part of the bill.

If you don't believe this, visit the American cemeteries on the battlefields abroad. Or visit any of the veterans' hospitals in the United States. On a tour of the country, in the midst of which I am at the time of this writing, I have visited eighteen government hospitals for veterans. In them are a total of about 50,000 destroyed men—men who were the pick of the nation eighteen years ago. The very able chief surgeon at the government hospital at Milwaukee, where there are 3,800 of the living dead, told me that mortality among veterans is three times as great as among those who stayed at home.

Boys with a normal viewpoint were taken out of the fields and offices and factories and classrooms and put into the ranks. There they were remolded; they were made over; they were made to "about face"; to regard murder as the order of the day. They were put shoulder to shoulder and, through mass psychology, they were entirely changed. We used them for a couple of years and trained them to think nothing at all of killing or of being killed.

Then, suddenly, we discharged them and told them to make another "about face"! This time they had to do their own readjusting, sans mass psychology, sans officers' aid and advice, sans nation-wide propaganda. We didn't need them any more. So we scattered them about without any "three-minute" or "Liberty Loan" speeches or parades.

Many, too many, of these fine young boys are eventually destroyed, mentally, because they could not make that final "about face" alone.

In the government hospital at Marion, Indiana, 1,800 of these boys are in pens! Five hundred of them in a barracks with steel bars and wires all around outside the buildings and on the porches. These already have been mentally destroyed. These boys don't even look like human beings. Oh, the looks on their faces! Physically, they are in good shape; mentally, they are gone.

There are thousands and thousands of these cases, and more and more are coming in all the time. The tremendous excitement of the war, the sudden cutting off of that excitement—the young boys couldn't stand it.

That's a part of the bill. So much for the dead—they have paid their part of the war profits. So much for the mentally and physically wounded—they are paying now their share of the war profits. But the others paid, too—they paid with heartbreaks when they tore themselves away from their firesides and their families to don the uniform of Uncle Sam—on which a profit had been made. They paid another part in the training camps where they were regimented and drilled while others took their jobs and their places in the lives of their communities. They paid for it in the trenches where they shot and were shot; where they went hungry for days at a time; where they slept in the mud and in the cold and in the rain—with the moans and shrieks of the dying for a horrible lullaby.

But don't forget—the soldier paid part of the dollars and cents bill too.

Up to and including the Spanish-American War, we had a prize system, and soldiers and sailors fought for money. During the Civil War they were paid bonuses, in many instances, before they went into service. The government, or states, paid as high as $1,200 for an enlistment. In the Spanish-American War they gave prize money. When we captured any vessels, the soldiers all got their share—at least, they were supposed to. Then it was found that we could reduce the cost of wars by taking all the prize money and keeping it, but conscripting the soldier anyway. Then the soldiers couldn't bargain for their labor. Everyone else could bargain, but the soldier couldn't.

Napoleon once said,

"All men are enamored of decorations... they positively hunger for them."

So, by developing the Napoleonic system—the medal business—the government learned it could get soldiers for less money, because the boys like to be decorated. Until the Civil War there were no medals. Then the Congressional Medal of Honor was handed out. It made enlistments easier. After the Civil War no new medals were issued until the Spanish-American War.

In the World War, we used propaganda to make the boys accept conscription. They were made to feel ashamed if they didn't join the army.

So vicious was this war propaganda that even God was brought into it. With few exceptions our clergymen joined in the clamor to kill, kill, kill. To kill the Germans. God is on our side... it is His will that the Germans be killed.

And in Germany, the good pastors called upon the Germans to kill the allies...to please the same God. That was a part of the general propaganda, built up to make people war conscious and murder conscious.

Beautiful ideals were painted for our boys who were sent out to die. This was the "war to end wars." This was the "war to make the world safe for democracy." No one told them that dollars and cents were the real reason. No one mentioned to them, as they marched away, that their going and their dying would mean huge war profits. No one told these American soldiers that they might be shot down by bullets made by their own brothers here. No one told them that the ships on which they were going to cross might be torpedoed by submarines built with United States patents. They were just told it was to be a "glorious adventure."

Thus, having stuffed patriotism down their throats, it was decided to make them help pay for the war, too. So, we gave them the large salary of $30 a month!

All they had to do for this munificent sum was to leave their dear ones behind, give up their jobs, lie in swampy trenches, eat canned willy (when they could get it) and kill and kill and kill... and be killed.

But wait!

Half of that wage (just a little more in a month than a riveter in a shipyard or a laborer in a munitions factory safe at home made in a day) was promptly taken from him to support his dependents, so that they would not become a charge upon his community. Then we made him pay what amounted to accident insurance—something the employer pays for in an enlightened state—and that cost him $6 a month. He had less than $9 a month left.

Then, the most crowning insolence of all—he was virtually blackjacked into paying for his own ammunition, clothing, and food by being made to buy Liberty Bonds at $100 and then we bought them back—when they came back from the war and couldn't find work—at $84 and $86. And the soldiers bought about $2,000,000,000 worth of those bonds!

Yes, the soldier pays the greater part of the bill. His family pays it too. They pay it in the same heart-break that he does. As he suffers, they suffer. At nights, as he lay in the trenches and watched shrapnel burst about him, they lay home in their beds and tossed sleeplessly—his father, his mother, his wife, his sisters, his brothers, his sons, and his daughters.

When he returned home minus an eye, or minus a leg or with his mind broken, they suffered too—as much as and even sometimes more than he. Yes, and they, too, contributed their dollars to the profits that the munitions makers and bankers and shipbuilders and the manufacturers and the speculators made. They, too, bought Liberty Bonds and contributed to the profit of the bankers after the Armistice in the hocus-pocus of manipulated Liberty Bond prices.

And even now the families of the wounded men and of the mentally broken and those who never were able to readjust themselves are still suffering and still paying.

CHAPTER FOUR

HOW TO SMASH THIS RACKET!

WELL, it's a racket, all right.

A few profit—and the many pay. But there is a way to stop it. You can't end it by disarmament conferences. You can't eliminate it by peace parlays at Geneva. Well-meaning but impractical groups can't wipe it out by resolutions. It can be smashed effectively only by taking the profit out of war.

The only way to smash this racket is to conscript capital and industry and labor before the nation's manhood can be conscripted. One month before the Government can conscript the young men of the nation—it must conscript capital and industry and labor. Let the officers and the directors and the high-powered executives of our armament factories and our steel companies and our munitions makers and our shipbuilders and our airplane builders and the manufacturers of all the other things that provide profit in war time as well as the bankers and the speculators, be conscripted—to get $30 a month, the same wage as the lads in the trenches get.

Let the workers in these plants get the same wages—all the workers, all presidents, all executives, all directors, all managers, all bankers—yes, and all generals and all admirals and all officers and all politicians and all government office holders—everyone in the nation to be restricted to a total monthly income not to exceed that paid to the soldier in the trenches!

Let all these kings and tycoons and masters of business and all those workers in industry and all our senators and governors and mayors pay half of their monthly $30 wage to their families and pay war risk insurance and buy Liberty Bonds.

Why shouldn't they?

They aren't running any risk of being killed or of having their bodies mangled or their minds shattered. They aren't sleeping in muddy trenches. They aren't hungry. The soldiers are!

Give capital and industry and labor thirty days to think it over and you will find, by that time, there will be no war. That will smash the war racket—that and nothing else.

Maybe I am a little too optimistic. Capital still has some say. So capital won't permit the taking of the profit out of war until the people—those who do the suffering and still pay the price—make up their minds that those they elect to office shall do their bidding, and not that of the profiteers.

Another step necessary in this flight to smash the war racket is a limited plebiscite to determine whether war should be declared. A plebiscite not of all the voters but merely of those who would be called upon to do the fighting and the dying. There wouldn't be very much sense in having the 76-year-old president of a munitions factory or the flat-footed head of an international banking firm or the cross-eyed manager of a uniform manufacturing plant—all of whom see visions of tremendous profits in the event of war—voting on whether the nation should go to war or not. They never would be called upon to shoulder arms—to sleep in a trench and to be shot. Only those who would be called upon to risk their lives for their country should have the privilege of voting to determine whether the nation should go to war.

There is ample precedent for restricting the voting to those affected. Many of our states have restrictions on those permitted to vote. In most, it is necessary to be able to read and write before you may vote. In some, you must own property. It would be a simple matter each year for the men coming of military age to register in their communities as they did in the draft during the World War and to be examined physically. Those who could pass and who would therefore be called upon to bear arms in the event of war would be eligible to vote in a limited plebiscite. They should be the ones to have the power to decide—and not a Congress few of whose members are within the age limit and fewer still of whom are in physical condition to bear arms. Only those who must suffer should have the right to vote.

A third step in this business of smashing the war racket is to make certain that our military forces are truly forces for defense only.

At each session of Congress the question of further naval appropriations comes up. The swivel-chair admirals of Washington (and there are always a lot of them) are very adroit lobbyists. And they are smart. They don't shout that "We need a lot of battleships to war on this nation or that nation." Oh, no. First of all, they let it be known that America is menaced by a great naval power. Almost any day, these admirals will tell you, the great fleet of this supposed enemy will strike suddenly and annihilate our 125,000,000 people. Just like that. Then they begin to cry for a larger navy. For what? To fight the enemy? Oh my, no. Oh, no. For defense purposes only.

Then, incidentally, they announce maneuvers in the Pacific. For defense. Uh, huh.

The Pacific is a great big ocean. We have a tremendous coastline on the Pacific. Will the maneuvers be off the coast, two or three hundred miles? Oh, no. The maneuvers will be two thousand, yes, perhaps even thirty-five hundred miles, off the coast.

The Japanese, a proud people, of course will be pleased beyond expression to see the United States fleet so close to Nippon's shores. Even as pleased as would be the residents of California were they to dimly discern, through the morning mist, the Japanese fleet playing at war games off Los Angeles.

The ships of our navy, it can be seen, should be specifically limited, by law, to within 200 miles of our coastline. Had that been the law in 1898 the Maine would never have gone to Havana Harbor. She never would have been blown up. There would have been no war with Spain with its attendant loss of life. Two hundred miles is ample, in the opinion of experts, for defense purposes. Our nation cannot start an offensive war if its ships can't go farther than 200 miles from the coastline. Planes might be permitted to go as far as 500 miles from the coast for purposes of reconnaissance. And the army should never leave the territorial limits of our nation.

To summarize: Three steps must be taken to smash the war racket.

We must take the profit out of war.

We must permit the youth of the land who would bear arms to decide whether or not there should be war.

We must limit our military forces to home defense purposes.

CHAPTER FIVE

TO HELL WITH WAR!

I AM not such a fool as to believe that war is a thing of the past. I know the people do not want war, but there is no use in saying we cannot be pushed into another war.

Looking back, Woodrow Wilson was re-elected president in 1916 on a platform that he had "kept us out of war" and on the implied promise that he would "keep us out of war." Yet, five months later he asked Congress to declare war on Germany.

In that five-month interval the people had not been asked whether they had changed their minds. The 4,000,000 young men who put on uniforms and marched or sailed away were not asked whether they wanted to go forth to suffer and to die.

Then what caused our government to change its mind so suddenly?

Money.

An allied commission, it may be recalled, came over shortly before the war declaration and called on the President. The President summoned a group of advisers. The head of the commission spoke. Stripped of its diplomatic language, this is what he told the President and his group:

> There is no use kidding ourselves any longer. The cause of the allies is lost. We now owe you (American bankers, American munitions makers, American manufacturers, American speculators, American exporters) five or six billion dollars.
>
> If we lose (and without the help of the United States we must lose) we, England, France and Italy, cannot pay back this money... and Germany won't.
>
> So...

Had secrecy been outlawed as far as war negotiations were concerned, and had the press been invited to be present at that conference, or had the radio been available to broadcast the proceedings, America never would have entered the World War. But this conference, like all war discussions, was shrouded in the utmost secrecy.

When our boys were sent off to war they were told it was a "war to make the world safe for democracy" and a "war to end all wars."

Well, eighteen years after, the world has less of a democracy than it had then. Besides, what business is it of ours whether Russia or Germany or England or France or Italy or Austria live under democracies or monarchies? Whether they are Fascists or Communists? Our problem is to preserve our own democracy.

And very little, if anything, has been accomplished to assure us that the World War was really the war to end all wars.

Yes, we have had disarmament conferences and limitations of arms conferences. They don't mean a thing. One has just failed; the results of another have been nullified. We send our professional soldiers and our sailors and our politicians and our diplomats to these conferences. And what happens?

The professional soldiers and sailors don't want to disarm. No admiral wants to be without a ship. No general wants to be without a command. Both mean men without jobs. They are not for disarmament. They cannot be for limitations of arms. And at all these conferences, lurking in the background but all-powerful, just the same, are the sinister agents of those who profit by war. They see to it that these conferences do not disarm or seriously limit armaments.

The chief aim of any power at any of these conferences has been not to achieve disarmament in order to prevent war but rather to endeavor to get more armament for itself and less for any potential foe.

There is only one way to disarm with any semblance of practicability. That is for all nations to get together and scrap every ship, every gun, every rifle, every tank, every war plane. Even this, if it were at all possible, would not be enough.

The next war, according to experts, will be fought not with battleships, not by artillery, not with rifles and not with guns. It will be fought with deadly chemicals and gases.

Secretly each nation is studying and perfecting newer and ghastlier means of annihilating its foes wholesale. Yes, ships will continue to get built, for the shipbuilders must make their profits. And guns still will be manufactured and powder and rifles will be made, for the munitions makers must make their huge profits. And the soldiers, of course, must wear uniforms, for the manufacturers must make their war profits too.

But victory or defeat will be determined by the skill and ingenuity of our scientists.

If we put them to work making poison gas and more and more fiendish mechanical and explosive instruments of destruction, they will have no time for the constructive job of building a greater prosperity for all peoples. By putting them to this useful job, we can all make more money out of peace than we can out of war—even the munition makers.

So ... I say, "TO HELL WITH WAR!"

General Butler says goodbye to his boys at the Quantico Marine Base.

AP news wire, September 23, 1931
(Courtesy of Jeff Roth)

COMMON SENSE NEUTRALITY

by Smedley D. Butler
Major General, United States Marines

(From the 1939 J.J. Little and Ives Company [New York] book compilation of non-interventionist essays and speeches by Dr. Harry Elmer Barnes, Dr. Charles A. Beard, Dr. Philip D. Bookstaber, Hon. William E. Borah, Rev. A. Herbert Haslam, Herbert Hoover, Jay C. Hormel, Col. Charles A. Lindbergh, Eleanor Roosevelt, Hon. Sumner Welles, and others.)

COMMON SENSE NEUTRALITY

Let's look over this European brawl and see where we stand on it or why we should stand anywhere on it for that matter.

First, let's see if we have contributed one single thing to cause it. Also let's see if even a part of the responsibility for it can be pinned on us. Finally, let's see if we have anything at all to do with it.

If we think it over calmly, we all know perfectly well that we did not have one solitary blessed thing to do with the making of the mess over there. And that there is no possible sane and logical reason why we should feel any impulse to take a hand in it.

Did we have anything to do with the promises Britain and France made to Poland? No, we didn't. Did we have anything to do with Hitler's land-grabbing? No, we didn't. Did we have anything to do with Britain and France declaring war on Germany? We certainly did not and were not even consulted.

These are some of the SMELLY things in this pit of European back-alley politics into which we will be sucked if we don't watch our step—if we are fools enough to allow ourselves to get all excited about this brawl that is going on over there, as such brawls have, almost since the dawn of history.

Before they started this row over land and natural resources, did they ask our advice or tell us their plans? Ask for our good wishes or even our opinion? No, they did not, and we neither advised nor encouraged them, so why should we get all stewed up about it and furnish the ammunition to keep it going? Just because people on the other side of the world insist on continuing their age-old practice of committing mass suicide, do we as a nation have to follow their example and blow out our brains, too?

Are we to adopt a policy of sitting around this European cockpit and going to the rescue of our favorite cocks whenever they get themselves into a fight they might not be able to win without us? Are we to become so entangled in European high-pressure politics that the main issue at our elections will be whether or not to allow political changes abroad? If we are to make it our practice to take part in these cockfights over there we should certainly vote on it—have it in all our national political platforms every time we have an election.

Twenty-five years ago we sold them munitions and then had to go abroad to bail out Britain and France, helped drench the gore-sodden fields of Europe with the blood of a quarter of a million of our finest boys—the pride of our manhood—helped sow the seeds of the present orgy—spent fifty billion dollars on that venture. Are we to keep on doing it?

Are WE to blame because Hitler built himself a great hair-trigger war machine that crushes everything in front of it? Are WE responsible that England and France did not build a machine to stop him? Are WE culpable in any way because Hitler started before the other side was ready? Provided Britain and France really want to stop Hitler, are WE to make up for their failure to prepare to do so by sticking out OUR necks?

Suppose you were walking down a strange street in a strange town in a strange country thousands of miles from your own home. You come across a brawl. You have no real interest in it. All of a sudden you hear one of the brawlers cry out, in your native tongue, as he swats his opponent: "I believe in Democracy." You don't know in the least what the fight is about but your sympathies are at once with this fellow who speaks your own language. The believer in Democracy sees you hesitate and shouts: "Come on and get in—we believe in the same things. Also don't forget, if this other fellow wins, you'll be next. You'd better come in now."

You reply, "No, I don't want to. I'm a stranger and don't want to get mixed up in this. I like you but not enough to get into a fight. I want to be neutral."

"All right," he says, "be neutral, but you can gather up all the stones, clubs and brickbats you can get hold of and sell them to me, I'll use them on the other fellow."

That's a swell way to be neutral, isn't it?

Do you really think that if you start handing your Democratic friend ammunition, you won't get into it, too? You can't help it, if he's losing, and if he wins, he will only call you a scab, say he could have won by himself anyhow, and declare that he owes you nothing. He will also hate you because you made money out of his necessity. So both sides will hate you. On the other hand, if you stay out of this fight, with which you have nothing to do with in the first place, the argument that if the other fellow wins, he will give you a good beating too, won't apply. You will have gone on with your own business, instead of butting into a fight where you did not belong, and better still, the winner won't find you right there on hand and ready to be chewed up next. You will be thousands of miles away and he will have to come after you.

They say—well, if the French and the British don't lick Hitler, he will come over here and jump on our necks. He'll be bombing our women and children and shelling our cities. Don't let anyone feed you that rot. It doesn't take military education to figure out what I am going to tell you:

It will take NOT LESS THAN ONE MILLION soldiers to invade the United States with any hope of success. These million men must come all at once. They must bring not less than SEVEN TONS OF BAGGAGE PER MAN. One million men, seven million tons of food, ammunition, whatnot. For instance, just ONE item: They must bring four hundred thousand vehicles alone; tractors, fifty gallons of gasoline per day for each vehicle for 270 days—that's nine months' supply. Why, there are not enough ships in the whole world, including our own—and we certainly wouldn't lend them ours—to carry that kind of expedition. And remember, these ships have to bring with them enough fuel to get back with—to make the round trips. We certainly aren't going to give them fuel over here to go home with. Any dumb cluck can see that.

But here's some more:

They've got to have harbors to lie in; docks on which to unload their stores. You know that you can't stop twenty-five miles out at sea, drop a fifty-ton armored tank overboard and tell it to swim ashore and meet you on Broadway. Remember, that with all the harbors, docks and ships of England and France at our disposal in the World War it took us nineteen months to get 1,900,000 men to France. And that though this expedition was headed for a friendly country and that all possible help on the other side was ours, it took months of preparation after the United States had actually declared war before it was safe to send the troops over. You know very well that we are not going to open our harbors to them, prepare docks for them and invite them in. New York is the only big one we have on this coast and to block New York harbor all you have to do is to dump two days' garbage in the channel, instead of hauling it out to sea.

Don't you see, it's all a question of supply—this invading business. Men and munitions always run out before the supply of men in exhausted?

Just figure it out for yourselves:

For every man at the front, you must ship every day of the year from your home depot a thousand pounds of supplies; food, ammunition, gasoline, clothing, medical supplies, engineering supplies, spare parts, etc., to say nothing of replacements of the above. If you have 200,000 men at the front, you will have 800,000 supplying them from the rear—and you will have to send them 100,000 tons of supplies every day.

Remember also, that for every thousand miles you go across water on an invading expedition into a hostile land, you must take with you ninety days' stores of all kinds. It is over 3,000 miles across the Atlantic—three times ninety is two hundred and seventy days—nine months. No, the supply of a European Army in America is out of the question, that is, an Army big enough to land here.

There is another thing to remember:

No fleet can operate more than 1500 miles from its base and Germany proper would be the base of a Hitler invading fleet. No. he couldn't get his fleet over here, or get it home again, if he did. But—they say—he might build a base somewhere in South America. Well, my friends, those who got up that little idea overlooked the fact that it is farther by a good deal from Berlin to South America than from Berlin to New York, so why invade America via South America? It doesn't make sense, for when Hitler got to South America, he would be a good deal farther away from us, than if he had come straight over from Berlin. So don't let that frighten you. It is all pure propaganda and insane to talk of Hitler invading us. And don't forget, too, that we have a Navy of our own and it's the best in the world, too.

Now, what about an aerial invasion? Well, Colonel Lindbergh and Eddie Rickenbacher, the two foremost fliers we have, already have told us it's ridiculous to talk of an invasion by air or to talk or think of bombing New York from Berlin. But suppose they do invent a plane that might be able to do it. That airplane has got to make the round trip, too. And without landing. With the fuel with which it started. And even if they build a plane that will do that, we have enough brains in this country to make some sort of machine that will destroy it before it hurts our women and children. And don't forget that we have an air force of our own, and a fine one too. So let's take one thing at a time.

This war's in Europe, it isn't over here. And it won't come over here unless we invite it. And the best way to invite it was to raise this embargo and sell bombs and ammunitions. They'll have the stamp of American makers on them and they have the R.S.V.P. that will bring about that invitation. An invitation to go over there and join in the mess.

Oh, but the bogey is that someone will come over here. Don't be alarmed. No one in Europe can afford to leave home. Why, if Hitler were to leave Germany with a million men to go anywhere, if he ever got back he'd find everybody speaking French or Russian. Those babies would move in on him while he was gone. No, there isn't a single crazy war dog that can come over here. We can build a defense of our own country that not even a rat, much less a mad dog, could creep through.

Let's be consistent. We cry to high heaven that we are a God-fearing and peace-loving nation and therefore we don't believe in shooting people, bombing their homes, knocking down their cities with cannon. And we really ARE a God-fearing and peace-loving people, but certainly it's un-Godly, hypocritical and unmanly of us to say to the British and the French:

Sure, we're against this fellow Hitler, but being God-fearing, WE can't shoot him, WE can't bomb him, but we'll be delighted to see YOU do it, and we'll furnish the guns and the bombs. That is, provided you pay us double what they're worth. And in order that there may be no mistake about it this time, you'll pay us in advance. You see we're against going to war ourselves, but we're not against your wars. You go ahead. WE'LL sell you the stuff.

The majority of the people of this country are against Hitler but don't want to get into this war in Europe. Our people think the best way to stay out of it is to be neutral. How is it proposed to stay neutral? Why, by regulating the sale of our products. It was satisfactorily proved that the sale of munitions to the Allies in 1914-15-16 got us into the World War. Now by selling again we run the same risks. If the sale of products has a tendency to involve us, certainly the more we sell, the greater the risk of getting in. The more we sell, the greater the business and the profits, and the greater the profits the greater our interest in the success of the customer. Our business slogan is: "The customer is always right." Isn't it?

The embargo on the sale of munitions certainly limited the volume of our sales. It most certainly cut out blood money. So why did we raise it—why did we open the gate and run greater risk? Why? To make sure that Hitler is licked. But then we would not be neutral and we have pinned our hopes of staying out on our being neutral. It certainly does not make sense: to raise the embargo and try to stay neutral at the same time.

Also the time has come when we have to answer the big question before us: How often are we going over there to bail out Europe? Will we have to do it every twenty-five years? In addition to going ourselves last time, are we going to send our children today, are we going to be ready to send our grandchildren twenty-five years from now? Isn't it time to make a stand about this thing here and now? Are we so vitally interested right now that we want to contribute five million of the finest and strongest boys that the great Mothers of America have produced? Are you mothers and fathers so deeply concerned that you want to furnish your sons?

Also, let's look at this question from a personal viewpoint, which is the only one that counts in the long run:

It's all very well and high sounding to say:

The Government declares war. To say helplessly: As individuals we have nothing to do with it, can't prevent it. But WHO ARE WE? Well, "WE" right now are the mothers and fathers of every able-bodied boy of military age in the United States. "WE" are also you young men of voting age and over, that they'll use for cannon fodder. And "WE" can prevent it.

Now—you MOTHERS, particularly:

The only way you can resist all this war hysteria and beating tomtoms is by hanging onto the love you bear your boys. When you listen to some well-worded, well-delivered war speech, just remember that it's nothing but Sound. It's your boy that matters. And no amount of sound can make up to you for the loss of your boy. After you've heard one of these speeches and your blood is all hot and you want to go and hit someone like Hitler—go upstairs where your boy is asleep. Go into his bedroom. You'll find him lying there, pillows all messed up, covers all tangled, sleeping away so hard. Look at him. Put your hand on that spot at the back of his beck, the place you used to love to kiss when he was a baby. Just stroke it a little. You won't wake him up, he knows it's you. Just look at his strong, fine, young body—because only the BEST boys are chosen for war. Look at this splendid young creature who's part of yourself. You brought him into the world. You cared for him. That boy relies on you. You taught him to do that, didn't you? Now I ask you: Are you going to run out on him? Are you going to let someone beat a drum or blow a bugle and make him chase after it and be killed or crippled on a foreign land? Are the Mothers of America ashamed to make this fight to stay out of this European War on the ground of their love for their sons—for what better ground could there be?

Have you ever been in one of those huge Veterans Hospitals it has been necessary to build to take care of the thousands of helpless and maimed cripples still with us from the LAST war? If you have, you will not need a reminder of what war can do to your boy, how it can render his life useless and broken at twenty, and yet keep him cruelly alive for the whole span of it. If you have not, I advise you to go and see one of them, for nothing could bring home to you more clearly or tragically the fact that in the last analysis it is your boy who is going to pay the piper. Few there are who come back entirely unscathed, and some come back in such a way that you would find yourself praying for their release from pain. Those withered, elderly, spiritless men who lie and sit so patiently in their wards day after day in those hospitals, waiting for the end, as they have waited since they got there twenty years ago, were the flower of our boys in their time. It is not age that has brought them to this pass, for their average age is a little over forty, it is WAR. Like the Unknown Soldier who was one of them, they too had mothers and fathers who felt toward them as you do about your boy. Thank God, this is a democracy, and by your voice and by your vote you can save your boy. You are the bosses of this country—you mothers, you fathers.

And that brings up another point:

If you let this country go into a European war, you will lose this democracy, don't forget that. As you stand by your boy in bed, he is safe, but here is another picture. It may help you to build up resistance against all this propaganda which will almost drown you.

Somewhere in a muddy trench, thousands of miles away from you and your home, your boy, the same one that is sleeping so sweetly and safely in his bed with you on his side, is waiting to "go over the top." Just before dawn. Drizzling rain. Dark and dismal. Face caked with mud and tears. So homesick and longing for you and home. Thinks of you on your knees praying for him. He is frightened to death, but still more scared the boy next to him will discover his terror. That's your boy. Stomach as big as an egg. I know, I've had that sensation many times.

Do you want him to be the next Unknown Soldier?

The Unknown Soldier had a mother, you know, and a father. He didn't just appear out of the air.

Do you want your boy, tangled in the barbed wire, or struggling for a last gasp of breath in a stinking trench somewhere abroad, do you want him to cry out: "Mother, Father, why did you let them do it?"

Think it over, my dear fellow Americans. Can't we be satisfied with defending our own homes, our own women, our own children? Right here in America? There are only two reasons why you should ever be asked to give your youngsters. One is defense of our homes. The other is the defense of our Bill of Rights and particularly the right to worship God as we see fit. Every other reason advanced for the murder of young men is a racket, pure and simple.

A Butler family photo of Smedley cradling his favorite cat.

(Courtesy of Molly Swanton)

AMENDMENT FOR PEACE

by Smedley D. Butler
Major General, United States Marines

(Originally printed in
Woman's Home Companion,
September, 1936.)

AMENDMENT FOR PEACE

I PROPOSE an Amendment for Peace, to the Constitution of the United States:

1. The removal of members of the land armed forces from within the continental limits of the United States and the Panama Canal Zone for any cause whatsoever is prohibited.

2. The vessels of the United States Navy, or of the other branches of the armed service, are hereby prohibited from steaming, for any reason whatsoever except on an errand of mercy, more than five hundred miles from our coast.

3. Aircraft of the Army, Navy and Marine Corps is hereby prohibited from flying, for any reason whatsoever, more than seven hundred and fifty miles beyond the coast of the United States. Such an amendment would be absolute guarantee to the women of America that their loved ones never would be sent overseas to be needlessly shot down in European or Asiatic or African wars that are no concern of our people.

SUCH an amendment, linked with adequate naval and military defenses at home, would guarantee everlasting peace to our nation.

How would such an amendment insure peace?

In the first place, the United States is in no danger whatever of military invasion. Even the Navy and Army Departments, which are always preparing for war, and the State Department, which is always talking about peace but thinking about war, agree on that. By reason of our geographical position, it is all but impossible for any foreign power to muster, transport and land sufficient troops on our shores for a successful invasion.

There is another bar to any invasion of the United States by the political dimensions abroad, which prohibit any one nation from leaving its own borders unguarded in order to make war on a foe three thousand or six thousand miles distant. Yet if, by some incomprehensible diplomatic hocus-pocus, an agreement could be reached among certain foreign powers whereby they would forget their own differences for the time being and pool their resources in a joint effort against the United States, there still would be very little fear of successful invasion.

Our fleet, bound by this Peace Amendment to stay close to home shores, would be on hand to repel such invasion at sea: if, through some serried of unforeseen circumstances and disasters, an enemy army did succeed in landing on our shores—the Atlantic, the Gulf of Mexico or the Pacific—the entire man power of this nation would spring to arms. Every American, every man and boy, would be ready, without conscription, without pleading—every American would be ready to grasp a rifle and rush forth to defend his home and his country.

Yes, everybody would be in that rush. Even the "peace at any price" people. They would forget their scruples. The pacifists would be among the first in line. The Quakers, the Mennonites and the members of other religious faiths which are opposed to the bearing of arms would be in that rush to protect our children and womenfolk.

History shows it. I know it from the experience of my own forefathers, who were FRIENDS.

Militarists and pacifists, Republicans and Democrats—all Americans, regardless of race, creed or color—regardless of political or economic beliefs—regardless of everything—all Americans would rush forth to defend their homeland.

Therefore, with the invasion of our shores an impossible military undertaking, the only war in which we can possibly become involved is one in which our people would have no interest and no concern—and no right to join.

It would be one into which we should be thrown by some economic, political or diplomatic intrigue, and not a war which we should wage in defense of our homes.

And it is from just such a war, a war such as the late World War, that we must protect ourselves. And from all the evidence, such a war is now imminent elsewhere.

Money—that's where we fit into the picture. Make no mistake about it. You can't fight wars without money. Everybody knows that. You can have all the airplanes and all the guns and all the warships and as many soldiers as you want, or as many as you can get, but you can't go to war without money. And remember. Uncle Sam has the money.

When the European powers get through their present task of "choosing up sides," and get down to the actual fighting, both sides will endeavor to maneuver the United States into the war—on their side.

ANOTHER question naturally presents itself: What of our territories and our dependencies? The answer is subject to great study and debate but let us note here a few points.

The Philippine Islands are now on their way to independence. They are not a defense necessity; commercially they are a liability; it is virtually impossible to defend them adequately. We should let them go. A bill to give Puerto Rico its independence has been introduced in Congress; we should let it go. The Virgin Islands, Guam, American Samoa, Wake and the Midway Islands are not indispensable to our national life. While American capital is invested in each instance, it would have to take its chances, just as in all external investments. The balance of trade is against the United States in all these dependencies—we buy more from each of them than we sell to them. They are not assets.

Hawaii and Alaska are our own territories: we cannot set them loose. It is virtually impossible, from a military or a naval standpoint, to defend them properly except at prohibitive cost, so I believe our defense of these territories would have to be by economic pressure. We would move the naval station and the huge military detachment from the Hawaiian Islands and such forces as we have in Alaska but we would announce to the world that these are ours and that they are not to be touched: that while we will not go abroad to fight for them, we will exact every possible economic pressure against any power which might be tempted to take these possessions. And the United States is so situated that it can successfully exert economic sanctions.

That leaves the Panama Canal Zone. The Canal is essential to our defense. We must defend it. Any notion which would attempt to block, damage or destroy the canal would do so only as a prelude to a war upon our people. We would defend it as we would any part of our coast.

We must always bear in mind that there is no royal road to peace. In recent years and as the result of disclosures of World War intrigues men and women have been endeavoring to chart new paths and byways toward the goal of peace. But no one of these paths, alone, leads permanently away from the danger of war.

These paths are neutrality, take-the-profit-out-of-war, referendum on war, total disarmament, mass protests, education of the masses, students' strikes and Oxford oaths. Let us suppose that all the antiwar measures that have been proposed were passed by Congress and placed on our statute books. Let us suppose that all America's youth of fighting age were to subscribe to the Oxford oath against participation in war.

THIS would not insure the peace of our nation. Laws passed by Congress in one week can be wiped off the statute books the next week. And laws can be evaded.

Take our neutrality measures, prohibiting the export of rifles, ammunition and other products to nations at war. There are ways and means of evading such embargoes. Machine guns can be—as they have been in the past—shipped as sewing machines. Cannons can be camouflaged as locomotive parts and, with the necessary bribes, placed aboard ship.

The proposed take-the-profit-out-of-war bill also could be evaded by intricate financial jugglery such as was common during the World War.

And last, even the war referendum—the plebiscite to decide whether our people are to go to war or not—is not foolproof. Don't you suppose that the American people could be roused, by skillful propaganda, to vote for a war in which we have no interest, even if a hysterical Congress did not previously wipe the law from the books?

Once the cannons begin booming and the drums begin rolling, red-blooded youth, despite its Oxford oaths, despite its massed protests, despite its satiric "veterans of future wars" will succumb to the war clamor. Radio orators screaming their pet and smug phrases of "war to end war" and "war to make democracy safe" and the newspapers shrieking in black headlines of war atrocities—these and similar propaganda arts of warmakers would be invoked to break down the earlier opposition of America's youth to war. You think it impossible?

Just look back to 1916 and 1917. In November 1916, Woodrow Wilson was re-elected president of the United States on a platform of "he kept us out of war." Five months later, on April 6, America declared war on Germany. Antiwar sentiment can be changed to a war clamor in a very brief time. But it takes at least nine months—that is the record for the prohibition amendment—for an amendment to be taken from the constitution, and one such as the proposed Amendment for Peace would take considerably longer. And in that period, surely we should return to our better sense.

At any rate, in the bitter fight that would develop in an effort to remove such an amendment from the constitution we would forget about the war overseas and keep the fight, with voice and ballot, right at home.

THERE is nothing un-American in the Peace Amendment. When our forefathers planned this government, they foresaw no necessity for preparing for wars in Europe: for wars that didn't concern us. As a matter of fact, after the Revolutionary War had been won and after the new United States Government was established, our army and navy were eliminated. There was no provision for an army or a navy. True, we had a militia. That is, each state had its own militia. We still have them. We call them National Guards now. But the militia, the only armed force in the United States at that time, was not to be used beyond the territorial limits of the United States.

If you look back into history, you will find that during the War of 1812 a certain regiment of militia marched northward toward Canada. When they reached the Canadian border they refused to cross, and went home. The militia then was for home defense—and home defense only.

That's what our army and our navy should be. Home defenders, ready and able to defend our homes, to defend us against attack—that's all.

The efficiency of our navy can be maintained by maneuvers a few hundred miles off our own coast just as well as it can be manipulated by maneuvers thousands of miles away, and almost in Japan's back yard, where our navy conducted its main maneuvers last year.

Let's pass all our suggested antiwar legislation, let's attend all the peace and disarmament conferences; let's have all the war protest meetings we can arrange; let our young men form their "veterans of future wars" groups—let's do all this and more; but if we really want to make it impossible to have our young men sent abroad to fight the wars of others, then let us by all means insist upon adding the Peace Amendment to the Constitution of the United States.

And the mothers, the wives and the sisters of the future cannon fodder must lead the way!

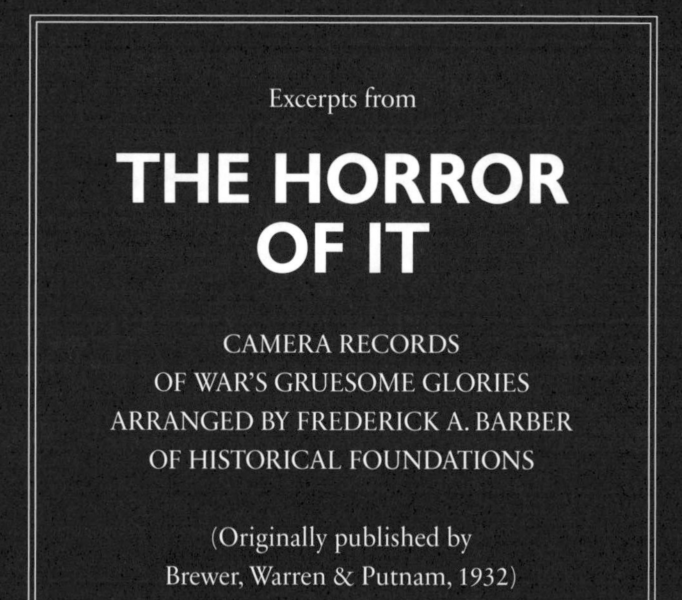
Excerpts from

THE HORROR OF IT

CAMERA RECORDS
OF WAR'S GRUESOME GLORIES
ARRANGED BY FREDERICK A. BARBER
OF HISTORICAL FOUNDATIONS

(Originally published by
Brewer, Warren & Putnam, 1932)

INTRODUCTION BY ADAM PARFREY

America's leaders had trouble explaining why an obtuse European conflict, later known as World War I, demanded citizens' bodies and money. Then flags started to unroll, drums started to beat, and posters began to reveal The Enemy, wearing Kaiser helmets, and spiriting away little girls still dressed in their nightclothes.

The propaganda was devastatingly effective. Few American males resisted the patriotic call of defending women and children, and did so in part by destroying The Enemy's women and children.

Years later, waking from the consequences of the Great War during the Great Depression, with friends and family shot or mustard-gassed to destruction, Americans began to realize that the war's victory was Pyrrhic, at best. Even so-called patriots began to wonder why it was deemed necessary to fight conflicts having little to do with a threat to American soil. Brigadier General Smedley Butler lectured to millions on why war was a racket. And a book called *The Horror of It* was published at the same time; its photographic record revealed the unacknowledged results of war propaganda's drumbeats.

It is no longer taboo to say that President Roosevelt required Pearl Harbor to drag a war-weary American public into supporting another World War. Discussion of FDR's foreknowledge of the Japanese attack is not only the subject of books by respected historians, but of documentaries on cable television.

War is more than a racket, it's an economic imperative which must be stimulated, however deviously. Smedley Butler speaks from experience of its primary beneficiaries; *The Horror of It* uncovers the results of propaganda's most vicious lies.

—Adam Parfrey

The Moving Finger writes; and having writ,
Moves on; nor all your Piety or Wit
Shall lure it back to cancel half a Line,
Nor all your Tears wash out a Word of it.

THOSE WHO WENT

AND NEVER CAME BACK

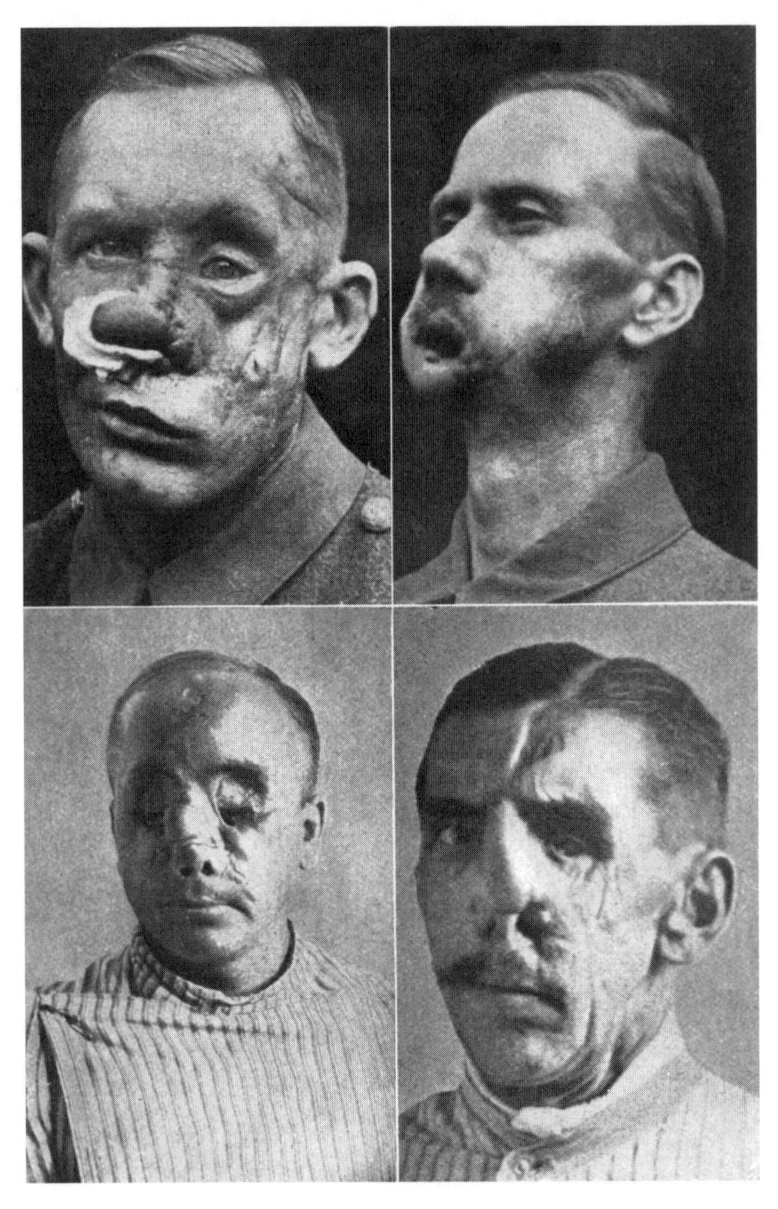

RECONSTRUCTION

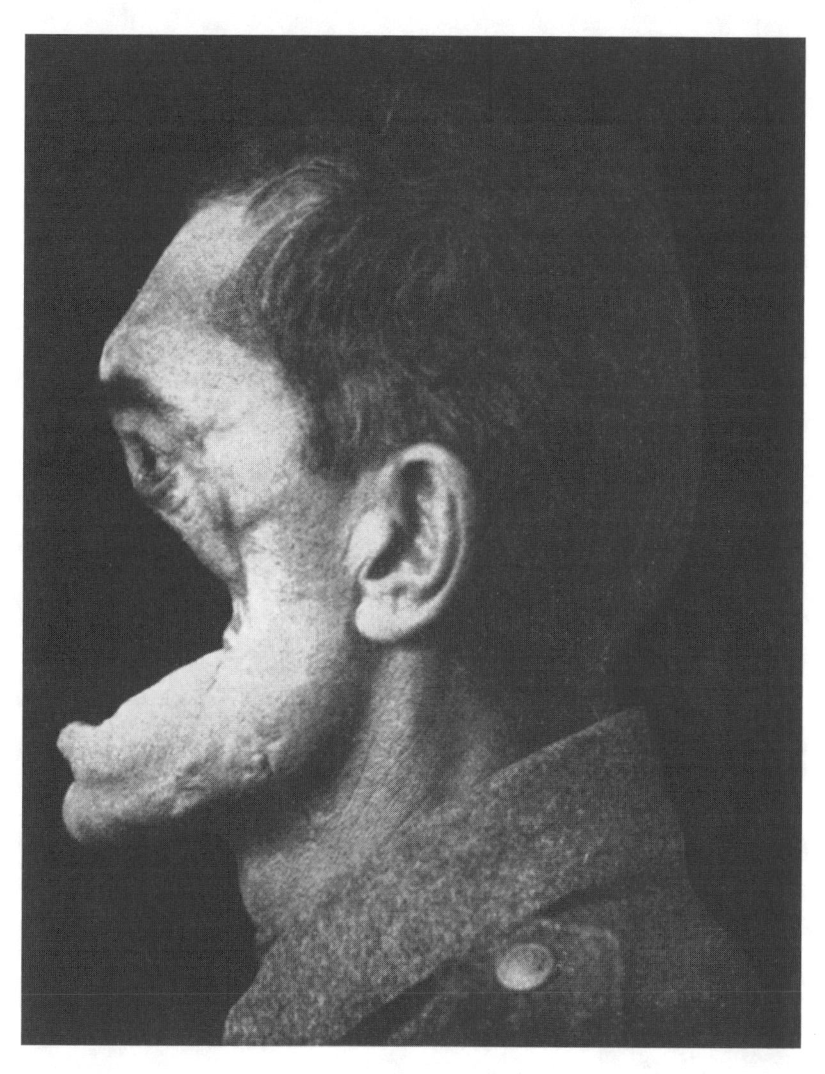

LIVING DEATH

LIFE'S BLOOD

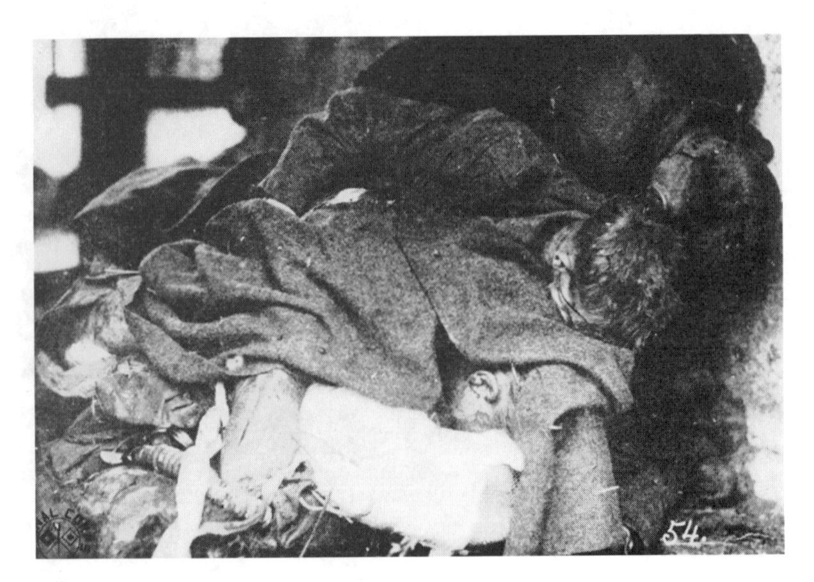

ASPHYXIATED

BIRDS

FLIES

WINDROW

TRANSPORT

THOROUGHFARE

ROADSIDE

HANGING

EXECUTION

NOOSES

OVERTAKEN

ON THE WIRE

SILENCE

THE NEST

FIELDS OF GLORY

WATERY GRAVE

LANDSCAPE

CITY STREET

STARVING

STARVED

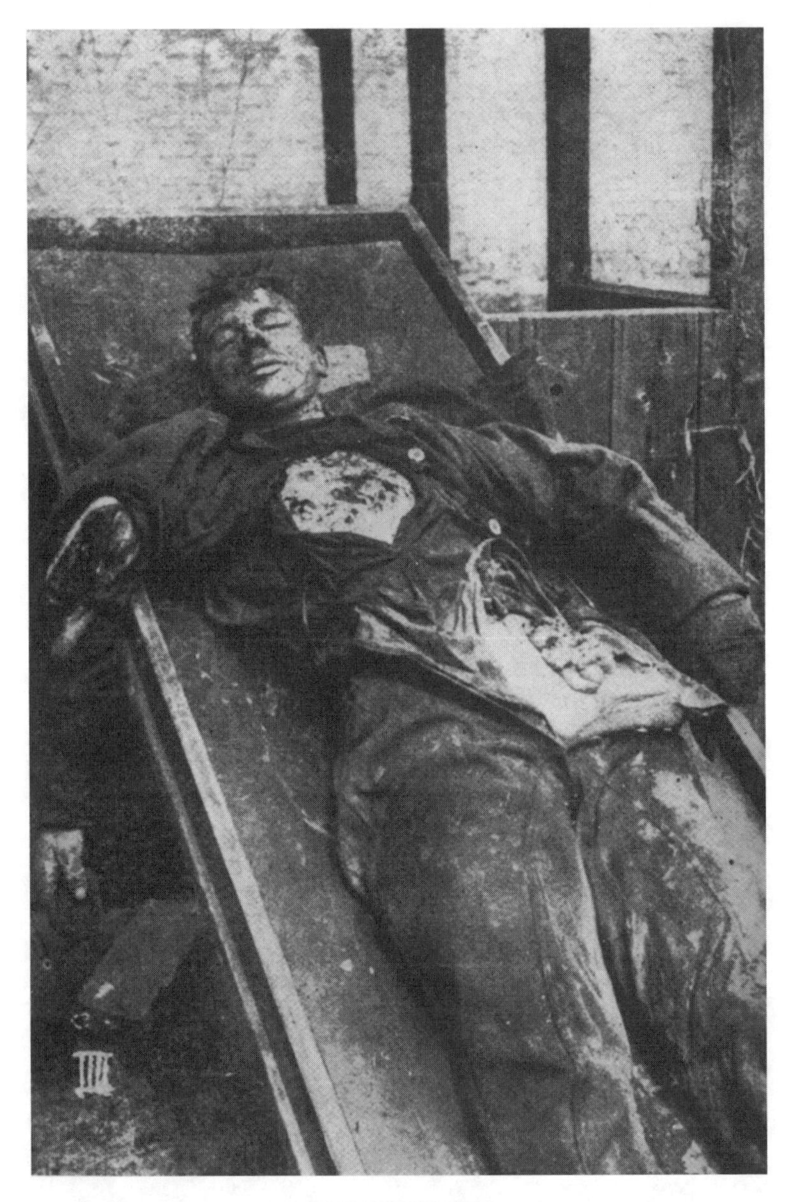

A MOTHER'S SON

CAUSE

EFFECT